T0114675

GODS BLUEPRINT FOR CHANGE

GODS NEW LAWS

JAN

BALBOA.PRESS

A DIVISION OF HAY HOUSE

Balboa Press books may be ordered through booksellers or by contacting:

Balboa Press
A Division of Hay House
1663 Liberty Drive
Bloomington, IN 47403
www.balboapress.com
844-682-1282

Because of the dynamic nature of the Internet, any web addresses or links contained in this book may have changed since publication and may no longer be valid. The views expressed in this work are solely those of the author and do not necessarily reflect the views of the publisher, and the publisher hereby disclaims any responsibility for them.

The author of this book does not dispense medical advice or prescribe the use of any technique as a form of treatment for physical, emotional, or medical problems without the advice of a physician, either directly or indirectly. The intent of the author is only to offer information of a general nature to help you in your quest for emotional and spiritual well-being. In the event you use any of the information in this book for yourself, which is your constitutional right, the author and the publisher assume no responsibility for your actions.

Any people depicted in stock imagery provided by Getty Images are models,
and such images are being used for illustrative purposes only.
Certain stock imagery © Getty Images.

Print information available on the last page.

ISBN: 979-8-7652-3492-1 (sc)
ISBN: 979-8-7652-3493-8 (e)

Balboa Press rev. date: 10/12/2022

FOREWORD

Jan is a woman of wisdom, integrity and compassion. She is completely devoted to her spiritual path. I have known Jan as a friend, spiritual mentor and powerful energy healer. Over the years Jan has used her phenomenal spiritual gifts to heal myself, friends and family members when no other recourse was available.

Jan has a deep and profound love of humanity and the earth. She spends much of each day sending healing energy to areas in need and to people who are suffering. Her gifts are truly amazing and are connected to Source. It is from a place of power, integrity and a profound vision that she shares of her knowing and wisdom. The messages from Spirit were channeled directly to her are now shared in this book of guidance for us all.

Read allowing the energy and truth to resonate within you.

Nettie Harland
Wise Woman – Healer

CHAPTER 1

Today is a glorious day as the messenger found all solutions to the interferences which were affecting the earth, and yes even my ability to help you.

The earth is not isolated in this universe, and there was a huge attack on it to control all aspects of life.

The messenger was gifted with a sight no one else has. That sight was focused on the workings of the universe. That combined with the extreme curiosity she was born with, has allowed her to follow abnormal patterns which should not have been there. The details of these things are not the focus in these writings although she has many personal writings of her own. We will only say that these abilities had put her in great danger until today. She has found the last 2 pieces and is now free to write my words without attacks and interferes which always make her check and recheck her accuracy. Today she is a clear vessel for my words, the Only God. As she writes my words the power of them will flow through the universe. This is not just for earth as there are many races of lifeforms. Most would look very strange to you, but they are intelligent with life missions of their own. They are now in harmony and are again pursuing their missions.

Most humans will never think about life missions, but all humans have them according to their abilities and spiritual evolution. As you grow spiritually you will be given a new task. For example, maybe your friends tell you all their secrets and know you can be trusted with not only the secret but knowing what to say without judgment. This is a form of love. Then you might find yourself in a similar situation to see if you can apply the same principles to yourself. If you can, you are now ready to grow to the next stage of development. If you could be with strangers who have harmed others; are you still without judgment? Can you still see divinity in these persons? Can you look beyond the actions and maybe see the soul damage? If so, you will once again remove this mission for another.

As you remove the missions the soul evolves bringing you closer to me. The evolution never stops but can stand still if your focus is on your physical life. Earth is a perfecting ground. You will keep returning until you have outgrown earth. These are always masters to teach and guide. You will know them because of their love and inability to fully fit in. Their most prized moments are spiritual. They socialize to leave love and healing wherever they go.

To become masters all life lessons are mastered. Upon death they still want to contribute, and some will choose to teach on earth. The numbers of masters are set. The bible speaks of this number, but the information is wrong. First because there is no heaven, and second because the masters have already grown beyond earth standards. The number is 144,000. My messenger is one of these, as are all prophets and messengers before her.

This messenger is the only one who has my permission to write my words. The last was around 20 years ago called "Conversations with God" Much has changed since then, and new words are needed. The soul evolution of humanity is now moving very rapidly, and chaos needs to be averted. There is a fire to change everything, but a plan is needed because of the domino effect. My words can be the blueprint for change. Listen wisely and learn.

CHAPTER 2

The first step you must take is to pray for the good of all humans. Do not even look at yourself. You will not be harmed, and fear has no place in the changes needed. When there is fear, you have separated yourself from me. You may think you have a better solution, but you cannot see the complete picture. There is only one solution, not 50 rules which apply to the one solution. No man should apply a rule to that which I write. Governments do not need to have discussions over the best way to do these things. Never can it be combined with other laws. I think you have heard you do not take from or add to Gods word.

There are thousands of causes, and we would never tell you to stop supporting and working for them. However, we will ask that you focus your prayers on this divine plan. Seal your prayers at the last with "In your name I pray. Amen" The more prayers the more power. The prayer could be simple as "Dear heavenly Father/Mother We ask for divine assistance in this stage of change. We ask for the highest good for all humanity. In your name we pray. Amen"

This time is very complicated as all aspects of society are affected. So, we begin with the least complicated and will see great results before the multifaceted areas are attempted.

Each chapter from here on will be dedicated to the areas in a precise order. At no time are you to jump ahead to the next area when the previous one is not solved and working smoothly. However, at no time are you to postpone the solutions. They will be straight forward and precise. Any person who attempts to stop my rules will be cursed and beyond redemption. Maybe you think you don't care, or you don't believe in this. But the effects will be immediate for all to see. Then you will believe. Now let's begin to truly renew the earth.

CHAPTER 3

First, we will work on the area of economics.

1. We will strip all privileges from the wealthy making an amount over the total budget of the local government where they live. All extra money will go into a fund for housing the poor and homeless. The poor will not pay rent but will be held responsible for the upkeep of the properties.

    The contractors will be held accountable for quality and pricing. You will be paid fairly, and any scamming will be seen, and the company will fall.

    The oversight of the properties will be under the local government and will be funded properly.

    Anyone attempting to take from the poor will be taking from me. Any poor person attempting to take advantage of this help will be held accountable to me.

    If someone living in these housings becomes able to support themselves then they should move on as there are always people less fortunate.

2. Working for the government is working for the people. If your heart is not there you are to remove yourselves. Unfortunately, this is most and there would be chaos if all left at once.

So, fill your contract and leave with dignity. Only those with their hearts open to the people will be supported in the future. Do not think you are with me when you continually push to take benefits for women, children and the elderly. These agendas are to be removed permanently, yes even abortion. Do not speak of them again but pray for all. Your religions have misled you if you think these people are less loved by me, and you cannot judge it. Those involved in the programs in these 3 areas should look at your hearts. If you find no compassion or love, then you need to find another area to work. The clients should not be made to feel small, or unworthy.

3. Next let us talk about public servants. They are always pushed and threatened by their superiors, and it is very important they are content in their jobs, as they are in the front, in the public eye. First, they are to be paid fairly as they are my soldiers who choose to do what they can for humanity. The stress from above many times will steal their joy and leave them empty. Second there needs to be communication from both sides with respect. Many ways to save money comes from the public servant. Thirdly your rules have made you ineffective. Your paperwork has doubled it. Keep only the necessary things. You have jobs for those who just make rules, now let them unmake them and find other areas for them to work.

4. This is for the health care workers. This area has shifted to a focus of money and is not effective for the persons who are ill. The messenger has stopped as she was a RN for 36 years. She knows many of my thoughts as they are hers. She wants this pure, so there will be a break. She is back and pure again. There are many different jobs available today in health field and I speak to all of them after addressing the privately owned hospitals with the management. Luxury built hospitals are a total waste and should stop now. They are being built for tax write offs and instead you should give your money to charity.

Hospitals should be cheerful with color, as color heals. Any energy healer can tell you this, and there will not be a huge expense. Every hospital should put resources and money to have adequate staff. The staff in contact with the clients have become so overwhelmed with paperwork that they have no time to even talk to the clients or families. In turn the staff goes home discontented and unfulfilled.

Here again they have jobs which only make rules and they need now to be unmade. This includes the organizations which guidelines the hospitals follow. Unmake them as they are based on the fear of lawsuits. The energy of lawsuits is now changed. No one will get rich from suing and will only receive medical expenses and transportation for as long as the client needs it. If there is wrongful death, then the wages of the client until the age of inability to work is paid to the family. Terms to be agreed upon, but preferably every month to 6 months.

The owners/management of the hospital cannot make more than the doctors on staff. The extra paid before will go into a world fund supporting the doctors in the fields of refugees and war. The management of the world fund will make a doctors wage also. You must be able to show details of supplies with fair cost and the signature of them being received.

Now let us speak of public health. Examine your hearts. Teach, teach, teach. If they don't understand you are to learn a new way. You cannot teach the average diet to a culture who do not eat these foods. Work with their food groups. Attempt to have their language, if you cannot, do as my messenger and use an interpreter. Language is truly not her gift.

Now let us speak of health care in general. Your focus is totally wrong. Your bodies are magnetic energies. If your focus was not money, you would allow energy healers into the hospitals as you would a priest or even a shaman. Greed and big business, along with religion has stopped most of the world from using herbalist and energy healers. Religion stepped into this when their healings sometimes allowed the clients to speak to their guides or even to me. The healings cleaned their spiritual body and contact was made with us. Some of the most famous healers from the past include Mohammad, Jesus, Moses, Solomon, Isiah, Krishna, and Buddha. Less famous are Marilyn Monroe, Buddy Holly, Art Garfunkel, Princess Diana and her son Harry. In the future the messenger will be the most famous as she has healed most of the world. Her intents are healing, she does not need to see you or know you.

All diseases in your world start as problems in the energy bodies. If it is corrected before it goes into the physical body, it can easily be destroyed. Once in the physical body it can be helped with multiple treatments. Insurance companies could save a fortune if they covered these healing modalities. This would also allow people to see the healer rather than going into the cycle of health care. The cycle is doctors, insurance, and pharmaceuticals. It is corrupt and if it is not cleaned up within the year, I will clean it. Once again, the executives should receive the salary of a staff doctor. The extra money can be given to the world fund to provide drugs and disaster relief all over the world. The pricing of prescriptions will be fixed within one year. It is robbery pure and simple and will not be tolerated.

5. This involves wages and benefits

Any person who employs workers is compelled to be fair. Look closely at this as the future of your company is on your conscious. I will not support any company who pays a wage so low that a person has to work 2 jobs to survive. Nor will I support one who works all at less than full time to avoid paying benefits. If you are not out there listening to your employees, then they are nothing but the means for a better life for yourselves. Every person is important and deserves satisfaction in their work. Every family deserves to be provided for.

Your wages should be a reflection of your skill and expertise. However, if you do not teach or help the employees with them, your wage should not reflect that. A fair guideline should be around 5 times the employees. Any extras should go into an education fund for underprivileged children.

6. Education

Schools who focus on sports leaving other studies without funds will correct this in 2 years. The coaches pay will reflect no more than double that of a tenured professor. Athletes will not be given money or cars. The money will be given to the professors of other areas equally and if they qualify for tenure, it is to be done.

Money raised at sports events will be divided equally to all departments for equipment needed.

The deans of the schools will receive wages of the coach plus another $200 a week. All extra funds raised will be put into the education fund.

Education funds will not be lowered again by governments. All supplies will be purchased in bulk by the state at a discounted price. All schools should have computers as you cannot elevate yourselves without it. A student should be able to buy a discounted computer over time.

Please open your minds and come from the love of learning. All problems can be solved. Once a year have all students participate in a state effort to send school supplies to other countries. It could be a separate part of the education fund. The messenger will tell you that paper is precious in Mexico. Money is raised every year for the students there, but it is not enough.

7. Banking is the most corrupt system affecting the economics.

First it is based on a system that in order to buy anything large you must have good credit. In order to have good credit you must keep loans going. If you pay cash for things you are penalized. You will reverse this. The client should be able to show income and receipts for things bought with cash.

Second, the banks have gotten extremely rich by charging interest rates that many cannot pay and many times will throw them into default, at which time you can repossess and resell it again.

The interest rates should never exceed 10%. This is for cards for credit also.

Third For all executives of the bank you may not have a salary greater than double that of the branch managers. Any excess money will be put back into the communities you serve. Because of the extreme level of corruption here the penalties of not abiding by my words will be severe. First you will look for loopholes, but I know your hearts and there will be no loophole you can hide from me. You have 6 months from the date the book is published. The 10% interest rate is true for all transactions of any kind. You should have less but never more.

8. City managers including mayors

From this point on you do not receive free cars, or vacations. You are in service to the people of the city. Your benefits are stripping the cities of vital services and will not be tolerated. Your salaries will not exceed that of a bank manager. The mayor will receive that plus $200 extra per week. The money saved will be put back into the education budget to pay your teachers a fair wage, if there is more put it into rebuilding your roads.

9. Housing

An average person cannot afford to own a house or a property. This is once again corruption within the real estate markets, and they are partnered with the loan companies. Many people in these fields do both sides. The housing cost within 2 years will be lowered 15% and at the end of 5 years will decrease another 15%. Those who already own will have their loans changed to reflect the new cost. Any equity paid will be honored. If the house is paid off and they sell at the new price the difference will be paid to them by the loan company.

You will badger these people into selling before the 2 years and will not be tolerated.

If you sell a loan to another loan company, you must be sure the owner is fully aware; by mail and phone call.

You cannot raise the interest rate above 3%.

Chapter 3

10. The central governments of the countries All persons in an appointed or elected position, excluding the president or prime minister.

You will hereby give up your free cars and proceed to rent them. Any government transportation of any kind will be paid for.

Your salaries will hereby be returned to 1982.

I gave the constitution to Jefferson Thomas over 200 years ago. I am now changing it. It has become a mess of rules and regulations which were not intended by me. The first thing is to remove everything from the original constitution but Medicare, Medicaid {Obamacare}, and Social Security. These areas are no longer open for discussion as they are protected by me. You have already harmed the people by allowing private insurance companies to participate and bribe. Obamacare will be fully integrated into Medicare by the end 2025. The copays for all will be $7. You will not turn this over to a collection agency. You do not shame people unable to pay. All prescriptions will be covered with no copays. All pharmaceutical companies will participate and will not withhold drugs.

The government will hereby make arrangement to repay the money taken from Social Security. You have 2 years to fully repay it.

Second you will hereby give up your offices and homes in DC and will return to the states in which you were elected There you will employ yourselves and help in the community. You will return to DC no more than 3 months out of the year for your committee meetings. You will receive a salary for the 3 months only. The salary will include moderate lodging and rental car. The total will not exceed $25.000 for the 3 months.

For those of you more interested in power of the position rather than the money, I now am setting term limits for you. The whole cannot stay longer than 2 terms. If you try you will not succeed.

Third, for any election no more can be spent than the salary of a staff doctor.

Forth, now to the original constitution. It was a different world then and I now will clarify my stand on bearing arms. At no time does anyone have the right to carry arms of any kind into populated areas. From this date to the release of this book, all who do will suffer. After the book, the person will suffer double. Don't challenge me.

Police etc. will keep their guns for now, but you will not be able to fire it unless you have my permission. Then the danger will be real.

The NRA is to be dissolved now with all money going to the victims of war. The public is not aware of their true purpose.

Fifth The military has bled all economics and it has no true oversight. All supplies will now be purchased through the government. All countries are to decrease their full-time soldiers to half by the end of 2025. The soldiers with time left will attempt to rebuild the areas they destroyed. If this is not possible or does not apply, then your talents will be used in some community services and paid by the military. War will no longer be supported under any means. Peace talks will now occur with my blessing and my firm hand. The conflicts will be resolved. Anyone with rank who loves war will be replaced. All companies making money from war will no longer be supported. All organizations who support war will dissolve.

Sixth The President and Prime Minister are the only ones entitled to transportation. In return they will rent cars for their families, and unofficial visitors. They need to remember at all times the people who elected them and be respectful of all persons. Never are you to attempt to separate or isolate any persons, even from other countries. I will never support the humiliation of Muslims or Mexicans. From this time forward if they are shown to be responsible citizens and are contributing to society, they are to be assisted to stay for fees less than $500. The present system is robbery. Nor should they have to leave their jobs and families to re-enter in debt. Let's not pretend that they are paid the same salaries with any benefits. Many have not had a vacation in years. Some will lose their jobs if they have to leave for the 1 week required.

Now for the Presidents who took their power through all means. I will no longer support your power if you can not make the lives of your people better. It can not be done through war and both sides will not be supported. You must talk and listen carefully. Find the means to create jobs and industry which will help support the economics. You must stop now the killing of your own people and help rebuild their homes.

Borders were never in my design and the only way I can support them is to have peaceful passage for all.

11. Now the final step of my economic plan. Taxes

No one is exempt from taxes. Taxes vary all over the world. Some countries have higher taxes because they provide more social services; some have higher taxes because of the corruption, or to support war.

The most corrupt in the world is in the USA. Only a portion of taxes paid even reach the government. You pay taxes to the IRS, which is not connected to the government, but is connected to the Federal Reserve Bank, which is also not connected to the government. There was supposed to be government oversight but was bribed away a long time ago.

First the IRS will be dissolved. Second the Federal Reserve Bank will close. All monies will go to the US Treasury. All states will benefit. The persons in the US Treasury who were bribed will step down and will be affected by me. The US Treasury will impose a flat tax of each worker at 13%. No one is separated out. Not even churches.

Churches and corporations will pay a flat rate of 10%.

Those disabled, retired, or in school will be exempt. If assets are involved and you are disabled or retired, you will pay 10%. By assets I am referring to rental properties, stocks, ownership in businesses etc.

The increase in revenue will be used to increase jobs, re-education programs and social services. Much is needed to help mothers with day care. Social programs for the elderly etc.

Canada

They have some great health care, but their elderly and retired suffer because of the inflated rate of rentals and housing in general. The taxes have made some people very rich, and they will be held accountable. Seniors once retired will have a 25% discount on their rent, and the excess taxes will build quality housing for a discounted price.

By 2025 taxes will drop to 28%. All other countries should look for corruption and should decrease their amounts to that also. You ask why not the USA? Because their over all pay rates are much lower.

PART II

CHAPTER 4

This will not be started until the economic section is completed and working smoothly; however you are on a deadline. Even with problems you should be able to have everything functioning within 3 years. So, by 2026 you will be able to begin this.

1. This will concern the opening of your borders. Crossing from one country to the next has become more and more hostile, and no way to greet your visitors. The countries do not own the earth, most borders were taken in war. As the time of war is over, the borders should be opened for all to travel freely. No government has the right to refuse passage to their own citizens, or the right to refuse visitors. The visitors will not be followed or falsely imprisoned for any reason other than violence or robbery. Prices of their services or purchases will remain the same as the locals who are citizens. At no time will the police stop them for bribes.

   The purchase of properties will be respected at the local rates. If they request extra things which are not in the local culture, it will of course be more, but it should be fair. There is no more room for greed.

The opening of the borders will allow the mixing of the cultures as you are all connected and loved by me. It is not the role of the visitors to attempt to change the cultures. All humans are evolving, and they will change on their own. Just your presence and different ways will show them another way to do things. The visitors need to consider that some of the ways of the locals will work better for them while in a different country.

While in another country you must abide by their laws.

2. No citizen should be threatened or harmed for speaking their thoughts. Words are powerful in all forms and thought should go into the message you want to speak about. If you come across angry or hateful the message could get lost. Respect the person you are speaking to, and the result will be different. Even if you get no satisfaction at the moment the seed is planted for their contemplation.

   All governments of all countries will listen to their citizens and do what is fair if possible. Any who will not listen will no longer be supported. You are responsible to me.

3. At no time can a country be influenced by religion. Religions intent is to worship me, it has no other authority. The intents to elevate the prophets of each religion to be worshipped is not acceptable to me. All came with my blessings to teach and change peoples' hearts to love. That is all. They all affected large numbers of people. Not one of them would have wanted what man has done. Other than the huge amount of violence done in their names, people have become separated, each

believing their prophet to be the only true one. They were all true and they spoke of the time they lived in. The messengers evolved as time passed. Now today once again there is another new message. There will not be another religion as I do no longer support any of them. All assets will be sold and the money will support the poor. There will be no more selling of icons, or other religious items.

Any religions with priest, preachers, or other leaders will disband. They will be held accountable for leading the people astray. There are a few gatherings based on love which gives the power of spiritual investigation to each person. All thoughts and questions are honored. These will be allowed to remain.

This messenger has my authority to write and speak for me. At no time are you to proceed to worship her. No picture of her will be displayed in your homes. With technology today you will be able to see her on video. No country can ban the watching of these videos, or the book with my words. The interpreters will be held accountable as never before. You will not change my words or leave anything out. If you do, you will see my wrath. If anything is added it will be immediate death upon you.

This book will be affordable to all as the messenger will not be paid. She does it with joy and love for humanity and is totally devoted to me.

In the past my messengers were tortured because of that love for me. But let it be known that anyone who attempts to harm any in the future will die instantly. She will contribute to the betterment of humanity until I decide to bring her back to me.

4. The marking of time is an illusion only to earth. All others do not know time. When asking for something do not think of time. Think in reality. For instance if you need a car think "I need a car in reality" If the item is large it may take more of your time, but it will be manifested if appropriate. I will never support anything with the base energies of greed, envy, jealousy, anger or resentment. Also, you can not longer harm another person but the thought will harm yourself. There have been people who take payment to harm others. Many people never believed in it, but it was in fact true.

As of this moment it will no longer happen.

5. The selling of goods is unequal. You are buying cheaper products and making as much as 50% profit from them. This is not a fair exchange. The profit which is fair should be around 30%. This will improve the flow of energy around you and the goods, and you will prosper. The right way to do business is to focus on the customers, who will in turn focus on you. When you consider yourselves connected to the people and community you will have more contentment. When you feel connected to me you feel loved.

Now let us once again speak to the banks. You made the changes I required. Now I wish you to add another service. You will now require a person qualified in taxes to show the people how to best save their money. The service will be provided for all and will be free of charge. You also do not encourage the saving of their money because no money is made on the interest. Now you should put the interest between 2 to 4%. When money is deposited in the form of checks you currently hold them for several days and the money is invested by you, then put back.

You will now change this to the deposited checks are immediately good. The savings you will invest, and part will be paid back to the client as interest.

6. The car business has long been an area of corruption. It has been a huge stress on the people who must have cars to get to work.

    First you have 3 years to lower the pricing on the cars by 30%.

    Second- All cars will have government insurance built into the payment. All will pay the same rate as the government. It will not be canceled for any reason, nor will you increase the rates. Be ready to comply in 1 year.

    Third- The loans on cars will be fixed at 6 %. In 2 years, all loans will be at least 4 years. The same is for used cars.

    Fourth- Another huge area of corruption is after an accident. From this point on all vehicles will be inspected by a state representative. No insurance company will be involved, nor body shops. If possible, the car will be fixed. If the damage is over 50% of the value, the car will be replaced at a similar value.

    Fifth- now that people are feeling in better control of their lives, we want to enrich the lives. To do that the focus will always be joy. Work is necessary to feel necessary, but it is still time away from friends and family, and the real sense of joy. Now I decree that the employee will have choices of when to fulfill their hours at work. There are a few jobs this is not always possible as for nurses. But nurses should be able to choose the number of hours per day. The managers are screaming right now but let the employees fill in the gaps. All nurses know you must be covered. Many older nurses needing less hours would work longer. Now they have no options.

36 hours is now full time with benefits.

With more time for their families, I wish families to come together for the evening meal. No phone calls or devices. Try sharing ideas, honor each other, and support each persons dreams. Bless your food before you eat it and watch the difference in how you feel. Bless each other for the following day and feel different again.

Sixth- Now for the other side of life, when you are elderly. Today the families are spread out and often the elderly are alone. This is unacceptable and nursing homes are to be used only as a last resort.

Each community should provide a meeting place for the elderly. Games should be provided as are snacks. Drinks could be bought at discount rates. Yes, I have nothing against alcohol as long as they are safe. I also have nothing against tobacco as I created it for your contemplation. Crafts could be done, or musicians brought in, whatever they want. This will be their place with their rules. Let them even do the planning of events. No liquor license will be required as it is them that will serve themselves.

Transportation will be provided if necessary and will be wheelchair accessible.

No one is denied for race, creed, or religion. No TV should be allowed.

7. Let us speak of that which is dear to my messengers heart. She has smoked since she was 14 years old. She tried several times to quit which was totally unsuccessful. The reason now she knows is because it is in her DNA to smoke. I tell you now as the Only god that all people have been lied to about smoking. It does not cause cancer or emphysema. Get your energies cleaned and you will never worry about either of these diseases. Indigent people have always used smoking in spiritual ceremony to assist in sending their prayers to my ears. That is not necessary, but spirit loves a ritual.

The bigger part of the lie is that the secondhand smoke is harmful to others. Now there are cities where you have to stay home to smoke. HMMM, maybe we should look at that. Look closely at the smokers left standing. They are intelligent and are trying not to offend anyone. They also have more brain activity as they contemplate a lot.

The smoking laws must be changed within the first month. Smoking allergies are really just irritation. The irritation would probably diminish if you changed your attitudes. If you absolutely don't want smoking in the building then a room needs to be added with good ventilation, light, and comfortable chairs. They should not have to go outside. All outside bans are gone totally, even for covered patios. The messenger just asked me about people with asthma, this condition has an emotional base and should be treated by a healer.

The push to separate the smokers was done to stop the ones with deep thoughts from influencing the rest of the population; the ones who they can control. Welcome them back and listen as they speak. Abuse and humiliation will not longer be tolerated for smokers. Smoking is allowed in buildings with the permission of the owner. All brands are now safe, and the sin taxes should be removed immediately, as there is no sin. The government will receive nothing, and there should be 30% profit only.

8. In the past pleasure was seen as a sin. I'm talking of touching another persons body. If there is honor and respect it is not only acceptable, it is my gift to you. The human body was designed with precision. The messenger is laughing because of her age, and the changes to her body. When 2 people are attracted to each other, there is a heart or soul connection. It is perfect when there is both. But all of these can not be denied. We would not make touch pleasurable then condemn you for touching. The only condemnation is when there is touch without agreement, or with abuse. These things will affect both in negative ways, and they will need healers to fix the damage.

The public show of affection is welcomed. The holding of hands or a kiss. Change your views, you will allow your children to watch a fight but not affection. Love is everything; open your hearts.

9. A persons inner beauty is what all should look for. I call it the reflected soul. It can fill a person up and make them contented to see it. To a much

greater percentage this is reflected by nurturing women. There is a large part of the world which has chosen that women should remain hidden. The culture has suffered because of this. From now on the women will choose what they wear. This will be honored and respected. The women hidden since puberty will be embarrassed but need to be supported. I dearly love them and wish for all to see my love in their faces. Their husbands might feel shame at first, that other men have looked at his wife face, but hear me clearly; this is not sexual and has nothing to do with sex. If she is married to you hopefully it is because that is where she wants to be, out of love. If she is not there for love, then show her love and see if there is a spiritual reason to remain together. Honor and respect is everything between 2 people. If they cannot be there than you must not stay together as it will hurt your souls and hearts.

10. At no time, under any circumstances can you stone a woman. Nor can you cut or mutilate her body. Her body was made by me, and she will return to me the same.

11. There are reasons for the orgasm of the man and woman. They are my gift to you as they can soothe the soul and make the feeling of love stronger for the partner. There are also physical reasons as they firm the muscles and strengthen the heart. Other reasons are clear as both become content and happy. It should be the focus of both partners and your bond will become stronger. It is blessed by me, the Only God. Listen to each other as you explore the body. No areas are taboo. There is no shame.

The messenger just pointed out that there will be humans totally devoted to me that will not follow this until the first 3 years are completed.

Those rules are for those in positions of power in your countries. As I am talking to families or partners, please use your common sense and begin now. All will benefit.

12. The positions of power over the public are to be controlled by time limits. Even the judges of the higher courts will only serve for 5 years. Even the appointments will have public input, emails will be set up to hear the public. I will know if this is honored. You will allow 3 weeks to review these before the decision is made.

    The power of the courts will be equal regarding conservatives and liberals. These terms are abhorrent to me, but you love to use them. If it is tied on the decision, I suggest you look at your own personal belief systems and do what is right in my eyes.

    The right to appeal must be allowed.

13. Lawyers will be looked at carefully as there are many bad decisions being made on the part of the clients. You make good money and spend little time in the name of justice. If you do not value justice, find another area to work in. All false threats to clients will stop. The trauma imposed upon the clients affect their souls and I will not allow it. It is your job to present all the clients qualities to a jury without speaking falsely. The attorneys on both sides cannot badger, or trick anyone on the stand. A full answer will now be heard by all judges. The element of all fear will be removed.

14. Immediately all states and countries will legalize marijuana. I created this herb to expand your mind and heal diseases. Common sense must

be used, and if you are unsafe out you may be fined but no more than a seat belt fine. No person will go to jail. All persons of 18 years old or older may grow one plant per family. I do not encourage younger people to smoke as your brain is still forming and it could slow your learning process.

All stores which sell it will decrease the profit to 30%.

No prescriptions will be required. Doctors will be held accountable if the results of studies on certain diseases are withheld from the patient in lieu of prescription drugs. Herbal answers are always better. Healers should also be promoted. There are thousands of studies already to prove their effectiveness.

15. Healers, chiropractors, acupuncture, massage therapist, shamans, medicine women and men etc. will be covered by government insurance. Healers do not have to be certified if they can submit 3-5 letters of effectiveness from clients who send their addresses and phone numbers. Fraud will not be tolerated, and you will suffer if you do not truly have these gifts. Healers is the USA and Canada will receive $50 per session. Other countries should see the healers provided for, even with barter. Barter is blessed everywhere.

16. Shaman and Medicine women and men

Your rituals are out of date and your powers are diminished. You are necessary for your tribes, and all people. I ask that you fast for 3 days to receive a new vision for ritual. Purify your body and your mind allowing no thoughts of anger, resentments, jealousy, or greed into your thoughts. If they come you must stop the fast for 3 days before you can try again. No judgment is placed on this as many of you have been affected by others. When you can perform the new ritual, your powers will be renewed. All persons should pray for them as they undergo this process. In the future you will not harm another person but give them to me.

As you know from the first 3 years, I will not allow abuse of power. Now I tell you there will no longer be any abuse due to gender race or creed. All persons will be paid the same as is set by that position. People should be compensated for years experience.

17. The government will ensure that running of the banks is to my standards. An audit will be conducted every 4–6 years without notice to the bank. They will look at the loans and denials. They will look at the salaries and expenditures. But all records will be made available. They will check to verify that the extra funds went to a legitimate fund for housing.

18. There will be no further need for schools to have a 3-month vacation as the children are bored and it is a hardship on the parents. 3 weeks will be given off. Children should be allowed to learn math, science, history, music or art, and should have a physical education period; not necessarily a sport but running and stamina building.

All teaching materials should be updated within 2 years. You are wasting their minds, as children today are much more intelligent. Look closely at your tests, is it more important to memorize dates, or should you now be asking what was learned from a certain period of time. We want to create thinkers not robots, or more computers. Teach them to solve the problems.

All children should be allowed an education without harassment or harm. Any government which denies this will be held accountable by me. Primitive cultures will not have access to books but can learn from the wise ones in the village. Time will be set aside for this.

At no time is hatred of other cultures to be taught. Remove your own hatred and learn to answer questions as honestly as you know. If you have no absolute knowledge, then say so.

If you have sons and daughters to educate in university the daughters will be educated first. The daughter is more vulnerable without the ability to support herself. In the past they were only allowed the option to marry, most of the time without love. This is not acceptable to me. Love should be present with any partner. There will remain areas of hardship where having a partner means survival, but there should always be respect and honor.

All around the world children are used as laborers. From this date on they can only work 4 hours. They should then have education and playtime.

All people should be taught to read and write, there would be many volunteers to help. But space should be provided. The ability to read will expand their minds and no one should be left ignorant. The materials available for reading cannot be from or about the government. There are many wonderful books and should not be controlled by religion or government.

English has become the national global language and all children should be taught if they are to interact with other cultures. I realize that some children will not be going outside their cultures.

Children are precious to me. Child pornography, slavery and any exploitation of them is forbidden and will be dealt with severely for all to see.

Women are revered by me. They are the givers of life. They were not put here on earth to be sexual objects. You will treat them with respect and dignity. All no time can you force a woman into a sexual encounter. The courts have chosen to ignore the pain of women so I will take the results back in my hands. My hands will not be gentle, and you will never have another chance to repeat your crime. This is true even if you are married. It is abuse of the human spirit as well as the physical body.

Now something which is not talked about at all. It is the abuse by females to young boys. The damage is the same to the boys. The penalty will be the same for these women. The numbers for these crimes are huge, much larger than you can conceive of. You have become perverse, and it will stop now. The traumas will be fixed on all so this sad cycle can stop.

All people from today will acknowledge the right to live in peace for all people. Any aggressors will be punished by me.

The gun laws will protect the people in th cites; as for rural people, guns will be carried only for hunting. They should not be openly carried. Guns in your homes for protection is permitted. Hunting is allowed if you are eating the meat. Meat is necessary for many body types. Those who are vegetarians need to accept this. Many vegetarians would be healthier if you ate meat occasionally. It is true that all animals should be killed in a humane way. You can also help by blessing your food before eating.

Many manipulations have been done to the studies of diets. Many times, you will crave what you need, yes, even chocolate. The best advice is to listen to your body but be honest with what you hear. All things should be in moderation.

Now let's speak of children, they are pure when they enter this world and are easily affected by energies in the home. If there is anger or fighting in the home, it will affect their nervous systems. Very loud music will do the same. Protect your children from these and if the child is nervous or unable to focus, please take them to an energy healer. Medicine will only provide drugs, and this is not acceptable.

People are unaware of the energy from a TV, but it affects all. It will create a numbing effect which is why people watch it until they fall asleep. Please restrict the time it is on to no more than 3 hours a day. The energy will accumulate in the brain waves creating a loss of focus on life. Here again the brain needs a healer to resolve this. Some say they don't watch it, but only have it on for the noise. The effect is the same.

It can also be the same for streaming videos on the computers. Everyone should learn to be quiet. It is difficult at first and a walk could help. A quiet mind is a peaceful mind.

Now let's talk about the relationships with your parents. Many of these are broken today because of energies put on the family worldwide. Many healers have worked on this including the messenger, but all should pray for a peaceful resolution. You need to understand that you reincarnate repeatedly with the same souls, they are called your tribe. You come together to help each other learn life lessons and then grow closer to me. If the problems are not resolved in this life, you will see the same problem in the next life, however the roles could be reversed to help you see the other side of the conflict.

The messenger was born with gifts and a high vibration. Her mother was fearful of her and exhausted attempting to keep up with her. Her curiosity was insatiable, always asking about the world around her. Her mother would fall into bed exhausted and unable to sleep. As the messenger grew her mother pushed away from physical contact as the energy felt like pain. The relationship was harmed in one way or another until her mother was in her 70's. Your mother broke her hip and had to stay with the messenger. At this time she learned that her daughter was following another religion from the Christian faith she was raised in. The mother attempted to threaten her with hell if she did not stop. The messenger stood her ground while honoring her mother, but refusing to fight. At another time her mother called her crazy for her beliefs. The messenger removed her glasses and stood in front of her mother.

She asked the mother to look closely in her eyes. She asked the mother if her eyes were the eyes of a crazy person. At that moment her mother felt the presence of me, the Only God. Her heart was transformed. From that time forward she honored her daughter and began reading many different religions books. She also investigated the channelings of Mother Mary and others. She died at 72, once again in love with me, with an open heart.

After all this time all should be willing to embrace love. Many are capable but not willing. They speak of things they must give up such as the remote, or time to do things they love, maybe travel they were denied, possibly school or careers. Maybe if you were willing to love again it could be different. Maybe both partners should be honored. As it is written so is the power and energy of change is taking place. No ones dreams should be taken. Most things can be fixed. Fix them together.

Love is not necessarily one man and one woman. Love is divine in that it is a heart and soul connection. It is genderless and crosses all lines previously drawn by man. There is no creed, religion, or race separating love. It is also likely that you will love more than one person. This is for women and men. There is no room for jealousy as this is divine. Both genders should be able to have multiple partners if they can be honored, respected and cherished. It will create new problems initially as schedules are worked out, but it is very possible.

Marriage will no longer be tied to the tax system. The taxes are a flat rate for each person.

If something changes and love is no longer felt, first see a healer to see if something is wrong. If there is still no love felt, release yourself with dignity and grace. At no time is there to be anger and court battles over children or things. Be fair in all things never leaving someone broken and destitute.

The accumulation of nice things is acceptable to me, but the loving of the things is not acceptable. Love is reserved for humans and if any human suffers because of your accumulation, it will be cursed to me. The energy of hoarding is the worst energy, as it is the total disregard of the principles of money. Money is not related to self-esteem or regard. It is related to the abundance I gave you on earth. Without movement of give and take the abundance is gone. So is the gratitude you feel when you receive it. The receiving of money is a direct path to abundance. The giving is a direct path to its blessings. Remember this always when someone less fortunate is around you.

The only time I will allow the accumulation of money without giving is to save for a large item which is necessary for your life, as a car.

No church will ever again ask for a percentage of your pay. Money is given always freely from the heart.

A time should be set aside each day to contemplate my mystery and to pray. You do not have to face a certain direction as I am everywhere. As you will no longer be worshipping any messenger or prophet you do not need to celebrate their birthdays or the days they died. Make your celebrations for peace and love. With the same paid time off.

I am the Only God. You will worship no one but me. The messengers and prophets all spoke the words I gave them. They all knew the danger of diminishing a prophet, but humanity has never learned to fully understand the trials and dangers even without the human intervention. There have been other life forms which have harmed them and every follower of the new laws. I won't discuss these reasons now, but this messenger should have died more than 50 times. She is amazing even to us. She heals and continues on to serve the earth and help humanity. She knows that justice will only be served by me. She has begged for it and prays constantly for it. These words will have no changes to them. They will go straight to the publisher, then she will check before the release to see nothing was done.

Now we will revert to the 2 largest religions on earth. First the Christian faith, over 2,000 years old. Very few people could read or write during that period. Most were Jewish scholars, those scholars at the time of Jesus were living around the main Jewish temples in Jerusalem. Most never met Jesus until he is in his 30s. No word came before him. He was always a spiritually gifted child, but it did not really get notice until he was in his 20s. His parents lived in Mesopotamia. He was born and raised in a village called Corinth. His parents were married 4 years before and he had an older brother. The names of his parents were correct. When he passed 30 we asked him to travel and tell the people of the new social laws. We call him the Master of Love. His mission was to preach about loving your neighbors and love of self. He did go to Jerusalem for Passover and was told to preach on the temple steps. He was very passionate that day and was arrested for disturbing the service in the temple. Before the day was done, he was in prison. He sat in prayer and the guard noticed how different he was from the other prisoners. After speaking with Jesus for a while the guards heart was opened. That night the guard helped him to escape. He did not die on the cross, he left Jerusalem and slowly made his was back home, preaching along the way. He married Mary Magdalene whose history was really of royal blood and had 3 children. Mary was important because she followed him. And she was a healer in her own right. Jesus and Mary were both Masters on earth.

As far as the apostles there were 3 men which followed him. Timothy, Paul, and Peter. After Jesus died naturally Paul wanted power and Peter wanted the message spread. They split ways. Within 9 years of his death, at the age of 50, Paul was building the first church which would become the Catholic church. Paul and Peter both could not write. So, the story of Jesus fell to later scholars in the Catholic church, usually bishops. They made it full of miracles, magic and mysticism. They lowered the status of women which has never been my words. It also has never been my word to put your belief in another human to guide your spiritual path. You are responsible and can not get to me through any human.

For your knowledge Peter talked in small groups which were called the Gnostics. Those groups were persecuted by Paul and the church. Timothy followed Mary Magdalene to France where her family was from. She preached and healed there until her death. Many know her today as the Black Madonna as she was dark skinned.

Mohammad was born to a prestigious family who had influence on their tribe. There were many wars between tribes, and he grew up as a warrior. When he was in his 30s, he began to have visions which showed a peaceful state between the tribes and a new alliance to the state of Saudi Arabia. He began speaking out on national pride, and unity in protecting the country. Most of the tribes began following him on this. Within 3 years he was in close contact with me the Only God. I gave him a new set of social laws as they had not been changed in 1500 years. Mohammad could neither read or write, so he had a scribe write them down. The words were taken to the spiritual centers and read aloud, with Mohammad present. The energy was positive, and many believed the words. That was in Mecca and the Islam faith was born. His mission lasted 6 years at which time he was killed because of jealousy. He had one faithful follower which was Ali. He was to carry the message, but he was killed also. The word fell into the hands of the mullahs which are a sect of an older branch of Shiites. They hid the words until they had changed the sections they wanted to change. 10 years later the words reappeared, but they were contaminated.

As the years pasted the power of the people was put into the hands of the mullahs, as the majority could neither read nor write. The power became the top priority and spiritual growth was lost. This proves again that it does not work to have another human to guide the spiritual path. The mullahs will now step down and, a new government will be chosen by the king. All spiritual things will be the responsibility of each individual.

Hear my words clearly now, that no human will be harmed in my name ever again. You will suffer greatly for all to see.

This concludes the personal section. Let us now look at your earth.

PART III

Prayer is important for others and no less important for the earth, oceans, plants, animals, and the air with the weather.

All of these parts have causes already in place, but prayers should be primary.

In the past all these areas have been manipulated with energy for a variety of reasons. Most have been destroyed by the messenger and helpers. All healers are welcome and encouraged to look at this. There are areas of high galactic energies. They are easy to see as there is no life on these patches of earth. Don't attempt to put your hands on these as you will be affected. Rather pray for the releasements of energies not of earth. There will not be new ones to appear.

1. Let's talk about the production of food. Most of the plants of earth are resilient. But some are so affected that they have become fragile. they are necessary to feed the population, so we would ask that more attention is placed on grains, rice, and fruits of all kinds.

2. Next the earth can be restored to living energy without the need for fertilizers. This has become a huge expense and contributed to the demise of the small farmer.

3. The earth was not created to be full of weeds and other plants which choke out other life. These plants were mutated by energies not of the earth. As a result, more chemicals were needed to grow crops. And finally, the crops themselves were interfered with so production went down, and some crops would not even grow in the same areas.

4. All of these things allowed the big corporations to come in and take over the production of food. With heavy discounts on the chemicals they have made heavy profits as they increased the cost of food. In the future these areas of manipulation of the energies will be reversed. The energy will again go to the smaller farmers who love to work the earth, and food prices will drop.

5. Genetic manipulation of the foods is a science. It is not all bad. More research needs to be done, but don't close your mind to it. We wish to see the old flavors of food come back.

6. More locations will be able to grow food. Start experimenting and see for yourself.

Ornamental plants- Humans are very visual, and beauty around them is excellent to lift the spirit and rejuvenate the soul. Flowering plants have diminished and now will be restored. You all buy plants every year to watch them not grow then finally die. The energy has been cleaned and they will thrive and be happy to receive your love. Yes, it is true they respond to love.

Let's talk about the oceans now. They are being rejuvenated now. The fish are rapidly multiplying. The messenger has been working on the ocean where she lives. She noticed 8 years ago the pelicans left. At the time she did not realize it was because of energies in the water. This year they returned, and she is smiling because she knows why.

The solution for the plastics in the oceans has been worked on for several years now and the solution will be seen before long. I would ask that you are more respectful about leaving anything behind in the oceans. They are part of you. Every creature in the ocean is precious to me.

Water of all kinds are precious and should be honored. Try blessing your water and watch what happens, even when watering your plants.

When you are looking at many of the earths problems they are usually energic. Healers will be necessary to correct them. All should say prayers for the earth, plants and animals.

Sometimes it is appropriate for a species of animal to die out. The cycles of life on earth will bring in new species as well. Some came from meteors which hit the earth. All are appropriate. If they can survive, they are appropriate.

Today people are more intelligent than any time in history. However, we were seeing a trend of less compassion and more anger. Alterations were made in the genetics to prevent this. Now we are witnessing a huge shift of consciousness and increasing spirituality. It is a beautiful thing to watch. I see a bright future for humanity as wars go away and we truly learn to value each other regardless of race, creed, religion, and gender. You were never meant to be separated by borders, and there is so many of them. When you look at another human look for me in their eyes. I hope I am reflected there.

There is another drug I wish to address. They are called hallucinogenics. There are several different ones, but all produce an altered state of consciousness. Colors and visions are seen. This is not a negative thing as there are spiritual things which can be learned. It is always a good idea to have someone with you for safety reasons. These are sacred plants which have been used by native people for centuries. No one should ever be jailed for this.

I finish these words now with total love for each one of you. However, as with a firm parent, I expect you to honor and obey me. If my admonishments were severe, it is because there is no room for negotiations. You will obey or you will see my wrath.

I expect obedience in all things, but the way is not that hard. I want all people happy and fulfilled.

PART IV

- If you remember that thoughts are energy, then you know that your thoughts can become reality in someone else's bodies. If angry and you send something, it can become undone by stating you will it to be undone and send love. When you see someone harmed by your uncontrolled thoughts you will fully realize the implications of poor self-control. If it was sent with direct intent or ritual, you will be as harmed as the victim, with the same malady. It is the right of God to fight fire with fire. Humans do not have this right.

- When spoken to about others you should ask them to stop. To harm anothers reputation without solid proof will harm both of you. When falsehoods are spoken against another person the energy of the words are taken into their bodies and does physical, emotional, and spiritual harm to them. For the person who speaks them there is a downward spiral to the soul and evolution cannot occur.

- When you envy the gifts of others it stops the development of your own gifts, Rather praise them and ask God to bless them. Envy is of the dark and is of the ego. The purpose of the ego is to separate you from humanity and prevents you from looking inside yourself. To develop your own gifts, you must ask God for them, spend time every day connecting with him me gratitude and respect. Meditation is not always quiet, and many cannot do it that way, just be open and follow what occurs naturally. Never fear for nothing is more powerful than God. You can always ask for his help, and it will be given.

- When cuss words are spoken even if not directed at any one person, they are energy which never dies. They mix with the energies of others and create more darkness on earth. It is called collective consciousness. It is possible to change the energy of these words spoken in haste by asking the energy be changed to love. Conscious intent is powerful and works immediately.

- When cheating you stop yourself from the opportunity to excel. Excelling is the means to building a healthy self-esteem. It also provides you an opportunity to build your discipline. These two qualities will allow you to function in a healthy manner on earth. They make your life easier. It is up to ourselves to create our own realities and there is no easy way to do that. Discipline is the only way to see the fulfillment of your dreams. When the basic needs of the human is not met self-esteem and discipline cannot be obtained. This should never occur on earth as it is abundant. As we are all connected, we should see that all are cared for, until they are able to create their own realities. When we help, the goal is to meet the basic needs, increase self-esteem and discipline. When stealing from someone else you affect the balance in both lives. You create more of a lack in your own life and a trauma in the life of the victim. It does not matter the size or value of the object. If you feel you do not have enough it should be corrected within yourself because there is enough abundance for everyone. This energy is new, and everyone should listen. You can have abundance in all areas of your life, change your beliefs.

- If you employ other people in your business, you have a moral obligation to them. There has been a huge shift in recent years to avoid the rightful benefits due an employee which increases the profits for the owners. This is an abuse and as you are in a position of power the abuse in Gods eyes are even greater. If a person works 4 or more hours a day for you, they should be paid for a full day whether 8 or 12 hours shifts. It needs to be considered that their personal lives are disrupted and there is little time with their families. The morale of the employee is your biggest asset as they will be more productive. For those innocent souls who are happy no matter what you give them, beware for your soul for God gave that innocence for a reason, and they are blessed. You are in a position to affect other lives and God will test you to see if you are worthy. All is not physical, look at other things around you. Money will never make you happy alone, but the giving back to the people in your charge will give contentment to your soul.

- Riot Rioting is not Gods energy as it is based on anger not justice. It will never accomplish justice. The anger which is provoked will smolder in the hearts of the participates and create permanent discontent.

- Look to God only. The normal man cannot be without bias, and he will teach these biases to others like it is supported by God. If it is divisive, hateful or separates you into a group, it is not of God. There are many paths to God, and all are equal. These laws of God are for all religions for there is no distinction in the basic message. That message is love of self and others. What changes are the social laws which must be changed as the human race evolves. Religious beliefs must change with evolution because all now are closer to God and many have his spiritual gifts. Your hearts have a knowledge of its own and when used together with the brain you can know the right things to do. Remember always that all are his children and there is nothing you can do to stop that. Hell was created by man to control the masses. Many were told they had **NO** access to God and needed to be guided. This was to further control them. The people who lead the people astray spiritually are to be condemned before God. If you are in charge of people spiritually and have not searched your own heart for the truth, do it now because when you read this, from this point on, you are accountable.

- At no time are political opinions to be brought into a spiritual meeting, as the concern should be only for spiritual contentment.

- God is not vengeful and would never harm you. Your life lessons were set up before you were ever born. You must look for the lesson, learn, and it will leave you. If you persist you create harder situations until it is learned. Once it is learned you will receive another lesson to learn. You will always be learning. You must always ask what else do I need to learn.

- Coveting belongings. Coveting is envy which is considered a dark energy. Dark energies have power when sent through thoughts or works.

They affect the energy of the person it is sent to and affects the soul of the one who sent it. It makes no difference if it is consciously sent or not. Ignorance of your thoughts is not excusable. The results will be the same. Learn to accept your reality and use your thoughts to bring the abundance you desire.

- No other God before me. This law is brought back not because of actual idols but of material things being worshipped. To worship material things is to create a vacuum which must be filled with more things. Beauty is necessary around us but has no value monetarily. You can love beautiful things but put them in perspective and know they are not necessary for your self-worth and placement in this world.

- Mean spirited – to harm Intending to harm another person is like harming yourself. You are all connected, and damage will occur to both. This is not just spiritually, but also physically, emotionally and mentally.

- Not judge- Judging another is putting yourself into a superior position which is not reality. No one person is better than another. In Gods eyes you are all equal and loved. It is more productive to look at your own life and make improvements there. Those who frequently judge others may be doing it so they don't have to look at themselves. This should be evaluated.

- Boundaries on love- Putting boundaries on love is like trying to harness the wind. Love is soul recognition and is not of earth. It knows no logic or reason, it just is. How is it possible for others to interfere or judge this. When others do interfere it causes extreme emotional pain which leaves scars on the energy bodies. Many people never even find love but stay in relationships for other reasons. It is their choice but it should never influence you judging others when they do it. For you have accepted it and chose not to look for love. Be happy for others for it is a sacred bond. The different kinds of relationships seen today have always been there, they are just in the light now for all to see. They are all appropriate as you have no control over soul recognition.

- Leading astray in search for God- Many people think they have the only way to God, and how arrogant is that. They are no better than the next, because you are all children of God and equally loved. Because of this each individual has their own distinct path to God. If you believe that a church creates one path for its members you are being deceived. There are no collective paths. Many are able to hear God and can give advice but there should be no judgement about the persons choice to pursue it. It may not be the correct choice for that person. If your words are to manipulate or control any aspects of their lives you will be held accountable before God. This includes advice about their personal lives and the choices they make. Money is never attached to the message of God. Persons may choose to donate to the leaders so they can spend their time in contemplation and visiting the sick and poor. The poor should be the primary focus of any organized religion, and the goals are how to elevate them out of poverty. The second focus is to assist the members to enter their own contemplations with God. Quiet periods are necessary for this, and it is easier for most to receive messages when gathered together to praise God.

- Not speak falsely- When you speak falsely to others it damages your spiritual energy body. Your spiritual body is eternal along with your soul, and the damage will be carried forward to your next life. That damage affects all aspects of the physical body, so you will see deformities and grave illnesses in the next lives. When you reach a point of enlightenment and speak the truth the next life will be whole again.

- Marry- The number to persons you can marry has never been based on God controlling love, but on the ability to provide for the families. The meaning of cherish is hold someone in high regard, to nurture, to hold close, and to respect. If you are not supporting your families, then it is a marriage only by the laws of man. You have ceremonies and legally record it for tax and inheritance right. The marriage in Gods eyes is confirmed when the persons make a firm commitment to be together. The human heart can fully love multiple persons as each partner will meet different needs. The marriage will dissolve when neither can cherish any longer. It is recommended that a years separation is tried before the divorce is filed. You currently have a version of these marriages on earth, but it is one sided. The woman has the same right to have multiple partners. The meaning of adultery has been misunderstood; it means having casual sex with a person you don't cherish. God does not approve of this. Jealousy has no place in love as you are together for the mutual right to cherish. You will never own another person.

- Path in other hands- Your spiritual path is personal and yours alone. This path was set before you were born. You agreed to this contract with God and no human can influence this for you. If you need guidance on this, you need to talk to God. Your spiritual gifts will determine how you receive this information. It may come in dreams or visions, or you may feel it in your chakras. The idea may suddenly drop into your consciousness, and you just know. All you need do is say "God show me my path." Include this in a prayer of gratitude and love. He will hear and when appropriate the answer will be given.

- Approach me with love. - Approaching God with anything other than these feeling will only harm you as you are a part of God. So, you would be attacking yourself, and disrespecting yourself. As a human you don't often see the big picture or understand the part that you yourself created Some things happen to learn, other things happen for someone's lesson. But evolution of the human spirituality does not occur on a nice smooth path in life. It is the trials in life which promote you spiritually, and this is the whole purpose of life on earth. It is a classroom, and it is about experiences. Before birth you were perfect and when you return to God you will be perfect again. But make no mistake, every one of you agreed to come to earth in the families and situations you are in, to have certain experiences which will further evolve the spirit if you can rise above the situation. Humans are very resourceful, and you can pull on an inner strength by asking for it. In this way a negative situation can be changed to create a person who is stronger, more focused, assertive, and more loving to self and others. With assistance all can rise above, but you must ask and look for ways to change things, and many times it is within yourselves.

- Thou shall not live in celibacy - Sexual energy is a creative energy which when activated and shared with another person it releases hormones which nourish the human brain, the organs, and the skin. In the universe it releases the highest vibration of love and compassion. When added to the collective consciousness it helps the evolution of the planet. It has been shown that celibacy for religious reasons does not work and the practice should be abolished immediately. It was never Gods law. It is true that withholding sex can create more personal power, but it originally was not devised for anything good. For instance, abstinence could be used for more creative processes in art, music, new ideas, inventions and spiritual quests. It should not be used full time though as it dulls the mind and ages the body. Today the cultures have taken Gods sacred gift and turned it into a negative thing, because it is meant to be special and should make you glow with optimism and vitality. The gift has been explored by men who are feeling nothing, or empty after sex. So, they believe if they have more sex it will satisfy them. But the satisfaction comes from soul contentment and that can never be obtained by having sex with someone you do not care for. They want love but do not know it, but when meaningless sex is put first the discontent felt by the soul may hide the possibility of love. It is not Gods law that you must be married to have sex, but for your own wellbeing you should care strongly for the person you are going to have sex with. When force or coercion is used to obtain sex, and it is used by both sexes, it damages you and the victim. You have taken a sacred gift of Gods and turned it dark. It is often repeated because they are still looking for the satisfaction of their soul. In reality they are losing the soul, as pieces of it break off and are lost. Society has been brainwashed to believe men cannot control their sexual urges, in reality men have never been shown what to do when the urges come. Turn it to physical or creative activity. Men have also been led to believe that women don't have the same urges which is totally not true. The difference is in the gender and most women want emotional connection with a sex partner. We know intuitively that when you have both it is satisfying. When two partners are happy in the relationship magic can happen sexually. If you are happy but the magic is not happening or impotence is a problem, both can be corrected by an energy healing. The meaningless sex before has put trauma in the cells of the body and in the soul. The soul must be fixed with love. The epidemic of impotence is not diet or physical, it is spiritual and will be corrected only in this way. With rape and incest healing can occur but once again, it can only be done by energy as the problems are on a spiritual level. With the victim the cells and souls are healed as above. Additionally, they will need to be balanced and grounded. Balance the body/soul and the body/spirit. For the offender clean the cells and soul, then heal it with love. They will need additional sessions for their emotional bodies. Additional trauma should be removed from the heart, or the heart cannot remain open. The result can be heart disease.

- Thou shall not kill – When you take someones life it affects all 4 energy bodies in you, as you are all connected. If you have been physically attacked and must kill to save your own life, you will still be affected. You will need energy healing to return to perfect health.

The PTSD that you are recognizing now is the effects of damaged energy bodies. The more sensitive a person is, meaning more evolved, the more damage you will see.

- Not bear arms- Carrying a gun other than to hunt for food carries a negative energy. That negative energy will attract other negative energy. You will eventually be finding your moods change, and you will be less optimistic. You will perceive things differently; this is new energy, and this is why there are more wrongful deaths in the news. Any person who interferes with the word of God is without support from God in all areas of his life. If you are military be aware that your energies are changing, and they will not support the carrying of arms. The leaders will feel this first, and more negotiations will occur. Middle ground must be found. For those of you who are affected the most, the ones doing the fighting, there will be concessions because you are following orders and healing will be given without you having to ask. Forgive yourselves and praise God for his generosity. As for policemen, order must be maintained, but you are affected in your duties. Healing will occur now automatically. As new energies take effect you will see no guns on the street and a disposal of arms should be set up as people will want to rid themselves of that energy. As soon as possible your arms should also be disposed of. They will not be needed. Your leaders will be given that insight when the time is appropriate.

- Use God to harm others - Religions are mans inventions to separate. God has sent many messengers which you call prophets. They are all of God and gave messages which were appropriate for their time. Words are energy and each one of them was given Gods power of the word. Eventually the power leaves the words, and another prophet comes. Every religion honors the prophet, which was never the intent of the prophet. They knew all things came from God. As we are now seeing the next prophet be aware that the power is of God. All prophets are human and therefore cannot obtain perfection on earth, an imperfect place. But all prophets have dedicated their lives to God even though it causes many hardships, and God has blessed them. The prophets are love, and to harm anyone from another religion is appalling in their eyes and the eyes of God. There are no contradictions in the religions, but the new prophets bring new laws. If you wish to identify with your current prophet, it is acceptable to God, but the new laws apply now.

Do not put women in a lower status- The divinity of women has been affected by man since the beginning. Words have been changed in the holy words to put them under man. This was never Gods intent as women have necessary qualities to make the earth a healthy, happy place. As seen in the current prophet, it is no longer acceptable. Normally women have greater intuition and are the teachers of the world. They should be consulted in all things affecting the world, for they will have the ability to see the effects on all and will not be willing to harm any. Some of the women in high positions have been brainwashed and should look inside to see their true beliefs and intents.

- Covering their beauty- If a woman chooses to cover her beauty it shall be honored, but at no time should anyone mandate what a woman is to wear. Women do have a responsibility to honor men and dress appropriately, and men have a responsibility to honor and respect women. The world needs a balance of male and female energies to right the wrongs on earth. Each has to change their thinking. You are responsible for your thoughts, and they can be changed with focus on them.

- Use sexual power to harm –

  We have spoken of this before, but it is necessary to say once again that if you are in a position of power over others, and their livelihood or wellbeing is in your hands, you are morally obligated to care for them in the eyes of God. At no time is it acceptable to use sex as a weapon to keep a job or position. Neither is it acceptable to use it for promotion.

- Take anything not given – To take or coerce someone to give without the total agreement of the other is to be considered as stealing. If it is a bargain between 2 with a threat attached, it is stealing. This includes nonphysical things also such as a vote, or support. It is against God and is perceived as a threat to free thinking. The only loyalty you should have is to your values and your heart. You have an obligation to your soul, and no one has the right to bring your destruction of your spirit, or your rational thinking.

- Don't leave children to investigate – Children have a pure soul and are open to the spiritual world. Many remember being there before going through the birth process here. Their imaginary friends are often their spirit guides. There should be open conversations about these because as they age the ability to hear could go away. You have been told the children are more spiritually aware than we are, but that is only because of our focus. All of humanity is advancing at this time because the mass collective consciousness is advancing and taking everyone else with it. Because of the immaturity of the childs mind it is necessary they have the wisdom and guidance from the parents or mentor. At no time should you belittle or stop their search as they will create a heaven on earth with our support. The children are pure and should be honored. They can teach us if we listen.

- Children as weapons – Children are pure love and should never be asked to choose sides in arguments or discourse. They cannot withhold their love from a person. It can cause great imbalance or even damage to their emotional bodies to do this. This damage can carry over to their relationships. All relationships are important to the child as that person has been placed in their lives by God either to learn from or to teach. The children killing other children were all weapons between 2 or more parties.

- Harm people with energy – There are 2 ways to harm people with energy. The first is unconscious. When someone gets angry and slashes out at another person, that intense emotion is sent to the other person and can be immediately felt. It affects the aura first by denting it, or even putting a hole. It then goes through the etheric and physical bodies and will put abnormal energies in the area struck. The weak areas will be hit first. The most common is the head and chest. This will also close the chakras which cause disease in the areas affected. The second way is deliberate with intent to harm. This way is usually with ritual. Most people do not believe "Black Magic, etc." really exist or works; but it is intensely emotional and is energy. It works extremely well and can kill if that is the intent. I call the ones who do this for a living a dark practitioner. They are not in the light but they are there. Most of the people affected are good people and all ask, "Why me, I don't hurt anyone." The answer is the darkness hates the light. Now according to the 1st law if you send dark energy with intent to harm you will receive the same energies that you sent. From this time forward you will also lose support in all areas of your lives. For those affected who have a lot of pain for no obvious reasons you need to see an energy healer. Medication or doctors cannot help this.

- Hoarding money – Hoarding more money than you use is not acceptable in Gods eyes. There should not be one person on earth who is starving, and hoarding is selfish and with no regards for others. There are organizations set up for the care of children. Adopting them through these groups is a great way to use your money and give your soul contentment. When you are generous to those in need you open the flow of energy for more money to come.

- Live in isolation – If the purpose of coming to earth is to have experiences, it is defeated when you are shut off from the world. You should have the flow of life around you. Isolating for brief periods is good to gain perspective and insights but then your knowledge should be given to others in the world. Living in isolation can also stall spiritual growth as you are in a protected place with all your needs met.

- Put all things on God – If you have tried your best to find solutions to your problems and cannot then ask for guidance. Insights will be received. God is not a quick fix for all things wrong in your lives. Look inside and make the changes. You must know yourselves.

- Not be idle – Idleness is the devils friend. Everyday should be used for good purpose. If you are not working outside your home, you should have work around your home. If you have no home, you should do something productive to try to obtain a home. If you are unable to work, use your mind to affect you in positive ways. Learn something or teach another, reach out to help someone else. God loves productive lives.

- Not live alone – This is referring to the persons whose to leave society and live isolated from everyone. It is not healthy mentally for that person and is no way helpful to anyone else. It is impossible to have experience which will lead to the growth of the soul.

- Use God to divide religions – God will not ever be used as a weapon, as he is unconditional love. He does not care which prophet you cherish, only that you follow the most recent laws. Religion must evolve with mankind, or it is dead. Living breathing things change and grow. Words are power and must reflect the world around us. How can God not address divorce when 50% of marriages end this way. God is striving for world peace; how can it be obtained when there is no peace in the homes. Find peace in your daily world first then watch it take over the world. There is only one religion and one God, there just happens to be different prophets. The most recent prophet from the Bahai Faith (approx. 250 years ago) honors all prophets, and in their houses of worship all religions are welcome. There are no preachers; they praise God, singing and reading from their holy books. In separate meetings they come together to discuss the words of the prophet, but each individual is responsible for their own spiritual growth. Today this is still true.

- Separation of classes – When you speak of separate classes you further the illusion that you are separated. In reality you are all connected through God. When one class has more than the other classes all are harmed. Jesus never said there would always be poor, those were mans words and the men were not poor. It is wrong to not assist everyone to a higher standard of living. When their basic needs are not met their souls can not evolve. So, their entire purpose of life is denied them.

- Not use Gods gifts to make money – Gods gifts were given to help mankind. These are psychics, feelers, seers, knowers, intuits, and healers. As these gifts are more common now, they need to be addressed. There is a responsibility with these gifts. Others privacy is important, and you should never intrude without permission. In the past many women were put to death as witches for these God given gifts. It was not for fear that this was done, but for control within church. The priest functioned as healers, but the motivation was money. The wise women were intruding in this and often treated people for free. At that time the priests began speaking of healings as the work of the devil, which is still heard today. In the name of God, they murdered millions of women who were blessed with Gods gifts. Today the gifts are common in men and women, and a new trend is taking place. The gifts are being used to make money through the stock market, gambling, and investments. This was never Gods intent and should not be done. If the gifts are used appropriately these services can be charged for as they have needs also. If you can not afford the service barter may be used.

- Not challenge God – Challenging God is challenging the very force which gave you life. All live because of his love. It is true that he doesn't get angry at you, but your circumstances could change so you can learn. The natural course is to evolve higher and closer to God. If you blame God for your circumstances, then you are forgetting that each person created their lives before they came. Change your belief that you are powerless and have no control. Then ask for guidance for new and better solutions. When in your personal power the windows open to change your lives. Each one of you are truly magnificent and are a piece of God himself. Take control of the lives, beliefs, and emotions and create a great life for yourselves and give thanks to God. The very act of gratitude to God can change your life alone. Gods hand can carry you when you need it and turning to him when in turmoil is an act of faith we will not forget. Do not consider this submission because your free will never be taken away. But if defiant the path can get rough, because you have severed yourself from God, not the other way around. He will never leave you.

- Not place others before God – God is the only power source, the prophets are given gifts but remember that they came from God. You do not pray to a prophet, and this should be made clear. There are major and minor prophets. The major ones have religions created around them. The minor ones have passed Gods messages along but only affected a more local population. Each prophet had a certain contract to fulfill, each building on the one before them. Not separate, but continuous. To put the power and the glory on the prophet is to forget where their power came from. Prophets would be honored but the praise should go to God which created it all. The prophet comes at a time when the world is weary and without hope. Their very presence changes the energy of the earth and provides hope. Beware of any who attempt to remove this hope. There were always disbelievers, and every prophet was tortured and killed because the disbelievers were in positions of power. The very deaths of the prophets gave their words more power and it could not be stopped by man. What followed then was man then took the words, manipulated them and gave people what they wanted to see. Most people could not read at that period of time. Today the word can be seen immediately, and it will be hard to manipulate the people. As these words are published take them into your hearts and decide if they resonate with you. You can no longer sit on the fence, you must choose light or dark, love or hate. God will no longer support your path, and it will become rough. This is not a punishment but a lesson, for not one person will be left behind in this glorious time where peace is possible on earth.

- Burden to others – If you have the capabilities to help the providers in your families then all other burdens should be removed from them. No longer does one person in a family do everything. This is stifling for their spiritual growth which will give them a sense of hopelessness. When the family acts like a unit and supports each other, the home is happier, and the children feel more connected. Do not ask others to do things that you can do for yourselves. This will increase your self-esteem and knowledge that you could survive on your own skills. Gender should never be considered unless the task requires more strength which the man usually has, or more intuition which the women usually have at this time. Laziness is counterproductive to your path and a hardship to others. You will find as you get older it will become more and more difficult to find happiness or love. At this point you have become a burden to yourselves.

- Manifest evil – Manifesting evil can come in many forms. Anytime a person or group purposefully leads you away from God and the truth, it is evil. This writer has been affected for the last four years to try to prevent Gods law from reaching you. These groups and persons will be accountable before God. But by my blessings and grace has she persisted and is able to bring his message to you. Be careful what you say or print without contemplation as the writer is not a superstar to be exploited. The will of God will prevail, and you need to understand the need for these words for the world at this time. To want the continued chaos and grief is even beyond Gods understanding and he will not be kind with you. To question is always reasonable but if you cannot hear or try to understand you are dead spiritually. The earth continues to vibrate higher and higher as the mass consciousness is screaming for peace, love, and unity. You can not stop that many people, they have spoken, and you must attempt to grow and understand. If you do not, your body will not be supported by this higher vibration, and it will become ill. All God asks is that you look and attempt to understand. The time of killing the messenger is long over and must not occur again. Many men will hate the messenger because she is a woman but be aware that the whole earth is now governed by feminine energy, which is the only way to bring peace. You cannot fight that.

- Not look outside but in – To look outside for answers is to pretend you have no power which is never the case. Understand that power is not force, but a reserve to be able to face anything, it is true that God never gives you more than you can handle. If a group is affected the whole group should participate in thoughtful solutions. Anger does no one any good, look for new ways to solve problems. Don't ignore the young people as they have great insight.

- God in vain – This is the same terminology as the Ten Commandments. It means using Gods name to damn someone in anger. This is an extreme offense to God and requires asking for forgiveness with complete sincerity.

- Interest on money – Collecting interest on money has become a single business, with no other services offered. The only way this type of business can succeed is to charge high interest rates. At the beginning of this practice, successful businessmen wanted to help others and they loaned at reasonable rates. This should be looked at again. Others in need of loans should not be supporting your business. No one should pay more than 4% for any loans. Any late fees should be shared at the beginning and should not be more than 1% of the payment due. Loaning money with the intent to harm them is not acceptable in the eyes of God. Many people have attempted to negotiate on late payments and the companies have refused to help. This practice must stop now. The policymakers will be held accountable before God. Help your communities by loaning locally and watch the communities flourish. It creates a flow of energy where it was stagnant before.

- Borrow money to live beyond your means - Borrowing money for non-essential things are not good practice as it creates an energy of want. It builds over time and creates discontent. If you wish a non -essential item, it is best to save for it. If any item feels like a burden, it is best to sell it and remove the burden from your spirit. The purpose of this life is to be happy, don't create your own burdens.

- Stock market - The stock market is dark energy and controlled by dark humans. To contribute to this is to put dark energies into your lives. It will affect the whole family and happiness will be hard to find. It is the way of energy to affect who ever touches it. If you already are in the stock market and heed this message, you may stop and ask God to remove the dark energy from the money and your family. He will know your intent.

- Include the world - The internet has brought the energies together and mixed them. So, you are all sharing energies more than ever. If you wish wellbeing for your country, you must wish it for the world before your country will realize it. You might dislike some aspects of a country or maybe the leader but the people in those countries have the same needs you do and may not be as fortunate as you. Bless all people and all countries and send love to troubled countries. Love is able to change all things. Love and compassion are the highest vibration and is closest to God. Attempt to stay in this vibration as much as possible and watch your life change for the better. There are others who think that hating a country does not affect that country, but it is energy and absolutely affect it. It will make things only worse. The more sending love the faster the changes for good will be.

- There is a reason for every race, color, and creed. God is a master planner, and the human is unable to see the entire big picture. Just know there are no mistakes and accept his plan. You cannot have it both ways. Either God is the creator of all and is infallible or he is not. You cannot take the pieces you want and leave the others. There are universal spiritual laws. To feel different in any way from someone from a different culture, race, religion, or gender is nonsense and is not the truth at all. When you truly look you will see the spark of God in them. Treat each other as that piece of God, honor and respect them.

- Not use laws to manipulate – Using the holy words of these laws to manipulate anyone is to condemn yourself. They are to instruct people everywhere to the intent of God today/ As of this date the laws are in place and valid. Let no man spit in the face of God. If you do not like the messenger, then you do not accept God who has sent her. There must be an attempt to end war worldwide and it can only be done through the feminine energy. Embrace her as Gods choice and know that she is blessed in all ways. If anyone attempts to harm her it will be immediate death, as the energies will no longer support martyrdom of the messenger.

- Investigate for the truth – You may not like change, but you will be unable to stop it. All energies and systems will change. God has decreed it. If the persons are harmed who are initiating the change, 10 will take their place. It is the most exciting time in the history of earth, and it should be a joy to watch it unfold. The way was set up to be easy, only people can make it hard. Don't see disaster when something falls, as it was meant to try to feel the excitement of what could be coming behind it. At the same time don't cheer because there are going to be innocent lives affected. Say a prayer for another job to be found and send love and compassion.

This concludes the laws for 2022.

Thence forth these words come only from the Only Living God. This vessel is now claimed by me as my only true prophet. She is endowed with my gifts and has earned this station. Having never questioned my commands she has fulfilled them all and has remained faithful.

ABOUT THE AUTHOR

By the age 0f 6 the author knew what her life mission was. She graduated from high school by the age of 16, and started nursing school by the age of 17. She worked as a RN for 36 years, using her ability to heal in the hospitals. After healing herself she began full time healing work. She had her spirit guides to guide her. God then had bigger plans for her. He asked her to write the new social laws for humanity, calling her his first daughter. Words are power and this book has Gods power in it.

Printed in the United States
by Baker & Taylor Publisher Services